PATHWAY BIBLE GUIDES

The Art of Living
PROVERBS

BY BRYSON SMITH

matthiasmedia

SYDNEY · YOUNGSTOWN

The Art of Living
Pathway Bible Guides: Proverbs
© Bryson Smith 2008

Matthias Media
(St Matthias Press Ltd ACN 067 558 365)
Email: info@matthiasmedia.com.au
Internet: www.matthiasmedia.com.au
Please visit our website for current postal and telephone contact information.

Matthias Media (USA)
Email: sales@matthiasmedia.com
Internet: www.matthiasmedia.com
Please visit our website for current postal and telephone contact information.

ISBN 978 1 921068 97 3

Cover design and typesetting by Matthias Media.
Series concept design by Lankshear Design.

CONTENTS

BEFORE YOU BEGIN

"How should I live my life?" This is a pertinent question not just for Christians but for non-Christians too, judging by the shelves and shelves of self-help books you see in your local bookstore, and the letters pages of certain magazines. There are people wanting advice about all sorts of things, like "Which job should I take?", "What should I say to my friend whose mother died recently?", "What's the best thing to do in this situation?", and so on. The answers come not just from self-help books and magazine columns, but from a variety of sources: your family, your friends, your colleagues, your minister and other people you respect. Some of it is common knowledge; some of it is folk wisdom. As the old sayings go, "Too many cooks spoil the broth", "A bird in the hand is worth two in the bush" and "Don't count your chickens before they hatch".

However, when it comes to the art of living, the book of Proverbs is really the best authority on how to live, because its wisdom is no less than the wisdom of God—the God who created it all and knows it all. Indeed, the most important lesson on wisdom that Proverbs has to teach can be found in the very first chapter: "The fear of the LORD is the beginning of knowledge" (Prov 1:7).

Proverbs is filled with rich instruction on how to live—how to spend our money, how to work, what to say (and how to say it) and a whole host of other topics. Because of who God is, certain types of behaviour are good and certain types of behaviour are bad. Because of the way he established the world, we can observe certain patterns about the way it works, reflect on them and then act accordingly. Proverbs offers instruction that will enable us to live stable, good, coherent and effective lives.

But Proverbs also acknowledges that there will always be a voice—the voice of folly—competing for our attention and seeking to lead us astray. The voice of folly comes in many disguises—some of which may not be immediately obvious to us. We must learn to recognize it and reject it for what it is, for the result of heeding it is always death and destruction.

That the message of Proverbs is an unpopular one in our society should be no surprise, for its message ultimately concerns the Lord Jesus Christ. In fearing the Lord, we are not just to fear any old god but the one "in whom are hidden all the treasures of wisdom and knowledge" (Col 2:3). Jesus, as God's king, has been endowed with all wisdom and understanding, which makes him the pre-eminent authority on wisdom—the only truly wise man. In fearing him, we come to understand the real purpose of life, and therefore the real goal of wisdom.

In these studies, we'll examine what the book of Proverbs means by 'wisdom' and how that wisdom applies to our lives. It is my prayer that as you discover wisdom's immeasurable value, you'll hold it near and dear, and let it shape your life. To possess wisdom is to understand the true art of living.

Bryson Smith
October 2007

1. THE GAINING OF WISDOM

Proverbs 1:1-6

 Getting started

What are some examples of good advice you have received from others? What made their advice so helpful?

💡 Light from the Word

Read Proverbs 1:1-6.

1. According to verses 2-5, what is the purpose of the book of Proverbs?

2. Verses 2-5 mention lots of things. What do you think is meant by the following?

   • wisdom

   • prudence

   • discretion

3. Do you think the things mentioned in verses 2-5 are popular or unpopular in today's world? Why?

4. Which of the things listed in question 2 would you like to have more of? Why?

5. Verse 6 alerts us to the fact that the book of Proverbs is going to contain a range of different types of expressions of wisdom (e.g. proverbs, sayings and riddles). How would you define each one?

• proverb

• saying (this is translated as 'parable' in the NIV)

• riddle

6. Who wrote this book, according to verse 1?

Read 1 Kings 4:29-34.

7. Why is Solomon a good person to learn about life from?

The connection between Solomon and wisdom is the start of an ongoing association in the Old Testament between wisdom and God's king. Read Isaiah 11:1-3.

8. These verses describe God's future king (i.e. Messiah or Christ)—the one who will rule Israel. What characteristics of this future king are similar to those in Proverbs 1:2-5?

The connection between wisdom and God's king reaches its most profound moment with the coming of Jesus Christ. Read Matthew 12:38-42.

9. If Jesus is even wiser than Solomon, how should we respond to what Jesus says?

 ## To finish

Are there certain things about following Jesus which don't make sense to the world, and which seem a bit silly to do? How does this study strengthen our trust in what Jesus says?

 ## Give thanks and pray

Thank God for the wonderful wisdom of our Lord Jesus. Ask him to give you the wisdom to be obedient to him.

2. THE BEGINNING OF WISDOM

Proverbs 1:7

 **Getting started**

Is it possible to be too flippant or too casual in the way we treat God? How would such an attitude show itself?

☀ Light from the Word

Read Proverbs 1:7.

1. What do you think it means to have the "fear of the LORD"?

2. Is the "fear of the LORD" different to being *frightened* of the Lord? How?

3. What is there about God to be fearful of?

4. What do you think the phrase "the beginning of knowledge" means?

5. Try to write out verse 7 in your own words.

6. Look up the following references as well: Proverbs 2:5, 3:7, 8:13, 9:10, 14:27, 15:16, 15:33, 16:6, 19:23, 22:4, 23:17, 24:21. List some of the consequences of having the "fear of the LORD". (To save time, you might like to divide these verses between individuals, or groups of two or three, and have people report back to the group what they have discovered.)

7. It's important to note that when Proverbs urges us to fear the Lord, it's always in small capitals: 'LORD'. Whenever 'LORD' appears in small capitals in our Bibles, it stands for Yahweh, the personal name of the God of Israel—the God who revealed himself as Yahweh to Moses at the burning bush (Exodus 3). In other words, when Proverbs tells us to fear God, it's not the fear of any old god you might happen to believe in; it's the fear of Yahweh, the God of Israel. This fear of Yahweh is the beginning of wisdom. How is this lesson different to what the world tells us?

Read Psalm 2.

8. In this psalm, people are to fear not just the Lord, but his Son and chosen king. Why?

9. Describe the lifestyle of someone who lives in fear of God's Son, Jesus Christ. Try and be as specific as you can.

 ## To finish

What are some of the ways in which you are tempted to 'fear' things and people other than Jesus Christ?

 ## Give thanks and pray

Ask God to fill you with a reverent fear of him and his Son.

3. THE VOICE OF WISDOM

Proverbs 9

 Getting started

Who out of the following list of people do you think would give the most reliable advice? Why?

politicians

teachers

friends

family members

talk show hosts

work colleagues

doctors

shop assistants

It may seem a little strange to jump ahead to chapter 9, but this chapter gives us a good summary of 1:8-9:18. In our next study, we'll go back and look at some of the lessons from the earlier chapters.

☀ Light from the Word

Read Proverbs 9:1-12.

1. What image is used to describe Wisdom in verses 1-3?

2. What invitation does Wisdom give in verses 4-6?

3. What main piece of advice does Wisdom offer about life in verse 10?

4. What are the consequences of following Wisdom (vv. 6, 11)?

Read Proverbs 9:13-18.

5. What image is used to describe Folly in verses 13-15? How is this image both similar and different to the one used for Wisdom?

6. What invitation does Folly give in verse 16?

7. What main piece of advice does Folly offer about life in verse 17? How does this advice reflect a failure to fear the Lord?

8. What are the consequences of following Folly (v. 18)? How do these consequences contrast with what Folly actually offers?

9. If you are feeling particularly creative, try drawing Wisdom and Folly as described in Proverbs 9.

Read Matthew 4:1-11.

10. We have seen that Folly (i.e. *not* living in the fear of the Lord) will eventually lead to destruction, even though it tempts us with sweet rewards. How is Jesus a good example of how to deal with the temptation of foolish living?

 ## To finish

Folly often tempts us with short-term worldly gains and experiences at the expense of long-term spiritual blessings. What are some ways that we can keep our focus as Christians?

 ## Give thanks and pray

Ask God for the insight and strength to recognize and resist the voice of Folly.

4. THE OPPOSITE OF WISDOM

Proverbs 1-8

 **Getting started**

When do you find it hardest to live in the fear of the Lord?

💡 Light from the Word

In our last study on Proverbs 9, we discovered that folly (i.e. *not* living in the fear of the Lord) will eventually lead to destruction, even though it tantalizes us with the prospect of sweet rewards. In this study, we will go back to some of the earlier chapters to think about some of the disguises that folly can try and tempt us with.

The voice of the sinner

Read Proverbs 1:10-19.

1. What is tempting about the voice of the sinner?

2. What are the consequences of behaving this way?

3. Are there particular areas of your life where you are tempted by the voice of the sinner? If so, how?

The voice of the adulteress

Read Proverbs 5.

4. What is tempting about the voice of the adulteress?

5. What are the consequences of behaving this way?

6. Are there particular areas of your life where you are tempted by the voice of the adulteress? If so, how?

The voice of the sluggard

Read Proverbs 6:6-11.

7. What is tempting about the voice of the sluggard?

8. What are the consequences of behaving this way?

9. Are there particular areas of your life where you are tempted by the voice of the sluggard? If so, how?

 ## To finish

What are some other 'voices' or examples of how Folly is seeking to tempt you in your life? What are some practical ways that we can help each other to resist her?

 ## Give thanks and pray

Look back at the 'Give thanks and pray' from the last study. Use it again as the basis for prayer, but this time try to be specific about the areas of your life in which Folly is presently tempting you.

5. THE PATTERNS OF WISDOM

Proverbs 16

Note: This study is quite a long one, so it would be particularly good to prepare in advance so you can get through the material more effectively in your group time.

 **Getting started**

"There is no rhyme or reason to life. It's all just chaos and chance!" What would you say in response to this?

💡 Light from the Word

In this study, Proverbs 16 is treated as a representative chapter of the entire section of chapters 10-29. Read Proverbs 16.

1. What is your overall impression of this chapter?

2. List the sorts of topics and subjects which are covered by these verses.

3. Is there any order or pattern to the way the topics are arranged?

4. Are there any verses which you find especially helpful or surprising? Why?

5. Many of the sayings in Proverbs stem from what the Lord is like—what he approves of, hates, commends, and so on. These sayings make a value judgement about what is the morally right or wrong way to live, based on who God is and his righteousness. What verses in chapter 16 (if any) lay down obligations about how we *must* live if we are to live in the fear of the Lord?

6. Many of the sayings in Proverbs are based on careful observations of what happens in life. These observations describe the way things usually happen in God's world without always making a value judgement on how right or wrong these regularities are. What verses in chapter 16 (if any) describe the way things *usually* happen without making any real value judgement?

7. It can be difficult sometimes to know whether a saying in Proverbs is a statement about what is always right and wrong (which we should therefore obey), or whether it is a wise observation about the way things usually go in our world (which we should therefore apply more carefully, depending on our circumstances). Some people find this a little disconcerting. However, it's helpful to remember that Proverbs *wants* us to think carefully about its sayings so that we might live wisely and well in the world as people who fear the Lord (Prov 1:4-6).

Are there any verses in Proverbs 16 where it's difficult to decide whether they are 'obligations' or 'observations'?

8. The many obligations and observations of life found in Proverbs 10-29 reflect the fact that this world is not completely chaotic. There are regularities and patterns in life. How does knowing Jesus help us to understand the pattern and purpose of this world even more (cf. Eph 1:9-10; Col 1:15-20, 2:2-3)?

 ## To finish

When is it hardest to believe that life has a pattern and order to it? How is Proverbs helpful for us during those times?

 ## Give thanks and pray

Thank God for creating this world with order and regularity.

6. THE LESSONS OF WISDOM

Proverbs 10-29

 Getting started

What are some examples of modern-day proverbs which, in your opinion, give some helpful insights into life (e.g. "Haste makes waste")?

💡 Light from the Word

In our last study, we discovered that the large middle section of Proverbs (chapters 10-29) provide us with many insights about how best to live this life. In this study, we will dip into these chapters to see what wisdom they offer on three important areas of life: wealth, words and work.

(To save time, you might like to divide into three smaller groups, take one topic each, and then report back at the end.)

Wealth

1. Read the following proverbs. What do you discover about how we should *earn* money?

   • Proverbs 12:11

   • Proverbs 13:11

   • Proverbs 28:20-22

2. Read the following proverbs. What do you discover about how we should *use* our money?

   • Proverbs 11:24-26

   • Proverbs 19:17

   • Proverbs 22:9

3. Read the following proverbs. What do you discover about how we should *think* about money?

• Proverbs 11:4, 18, 28

• Proverbs 16:8, 16

• Proverbs 23:4-5

Words

4. Read the following proverbs. What do you discover about the *importance* of our words?

• Proverbs 11:9

• Proverbs 12:18

• Proverbs 15:4

5. Read the following proverbs. What do you discover about the way we *should* speak?

- Proverbs 10:19

- Proverbs 15:1-2

- Proverbs 16:23-24

6. Read the following proverbs. What do you discover about the way we *shouldn't* speak?

- Proverbs 16:28

- Proverbs 17:4, 9

- Proverbs 26:28

Work

7. Read the following proverbs. What do you discover about the *dangers* of laziness?

   • Proverbs 14:23

   • Proverbs 19:15

   • Proverbs 20:4, 13

8. Read the following proverbs. What do you discover about the *benefits* of hard work?

   • Proverbs 10:5

   • Proverbs 20:13

   • Proverbs 27:18, 23-27

9. Read the following proverbs. What do you discover about the *manner* in which we should work?

• Proverbs 10:9, 16

• Proverbs 11:1, 18

• Proverbs 15:27

 ## To finish

How does knowing Jesus and following him as our king reinforce the lessons we have learned in this study?

 ## Give thanks and pray

Thank God for giving us his wisdom which shows us how we should live. Ask him to give you strength to live a life full of integrity, wisdom and diligence.

7. THE SEARCH FOR WISDOM

Proverbs 30

 **Getting started**

Do you think that Christians are wiser than other people?

☀ Light from the Word

Read Proverbs 30:1-4.

1. In this section, we meet a man searching for wisdom in life. What is his name and how does he describe himself?

2. Possibly the best translation of verse 1 is the one mentioned in the footnotes of the ESV (and NIV). In other words, Agur is "of Massa", an Ishmaelite clan (cf. Gen 25:14). How does this make sense of verse 3? (Hint: look at what the apostle Paul says about the predicament of Gentiles in Ephesians 2:11-12.)

3. In his search for wisdom, Agur calls out for help from a competent teacher. What characteristics does he think this teacher should have (v. 4)?

4. Who would qualify to be Agur's teacher?

Read Proverbs 30:5-9.

5. How does Agur describe the word of God?

6. Interestingly, verse 5 is a quote from Psalm 18:30, and verse 6 is a very strong echo of Deuteronomy 4:2. What does this show us about where Agur found answers to his search for wisdom?

7. From what you have discovered about Agur, do you think that he has the "fear of the LORD" (Prov 1:7)? What makes you think this?

Read Proverbs 30:7-33.

8. In the remainder of the chapter, Agur offers different insights he has gained from having come to see that the word of God proves true. In general terms, what sorts of topics does Agur cover? (Some of these sayings can seem a little obscure so don't worry too much if you can't follow absolutely everything that's said; you're in good company.)

9. What lessons (if any) are repeated from earlier chapters of Proverbs?

 ## To finish

Proverbs 30 provides us with a wonderful case study of a person who has only been able to make sense of life by coming to know the true and living God. How has his experience been reflected in your own life?

 ## Give thanks and pray

Thank God for lavishing his grace upon us "in all wisdom and insight making known to us the mystery of his will, according to his purpose, which he set forth in Christ" (Eph 1:8-9).

8. LADY WISDOM

Proverbs 31:10-31

 **Getting started**

What do you think life would be like if you put into practice all the lessons we've discovered so far in Proverbs?

This final section of Proverbs is a poem written in the form of an acrostic. Each line of these verses in Hebrew begins with the next letter of the Hebrew alphabet: the first word of verse 10 starts with the Hebrew equivalent of 'A', the first word of verse 11 starts with the Hebrew equivalent of 'B', and so on, all the way to verse 31 which begins with the Hebrew equivalent of 'Z'. This acrostic structure highlights that these final verses are a summary of everything that has gone before them: here at the end of the book, we quite literally have the A-Z of Proverbs. In our final study, we'll investigate how this vivid description of an "excellent wife" forms an effective summary for the whole of Proverbs.

Light from the Word

Read Proverbs 31:10-31.

1. In study 1, we discovered that the book of Proverbs can help us live a wise, righteous and prudent life (1:2-4). How does the "excellent wife" of Proverbs 31 exemplify each of these qualities?

   • wisdom

   • prudence

   • discretion

2. In study 2, we learned that the "fear of the LORD is the beginning of knowledge" (1:7). How does the "excellent wife" demonstrate this?

3. In study 3, we saw wisdom described as a woman. What are the similarities between the description of wisdom in Proverbs 9:1-12 and the description of wisdom in Proverbs 31:10-31?

4. In study 4, we were given advice about the foolishness of the sinner, the adulteress and the sluggard. How is the "excellent wife" the exact opposite of each of these three types of people?

   • the sinner

   • the adulteress

   • the sluggard

5. In study 6, we were given life lessons about wealth, words and work. How does the "excellent wife" exemplify those lessons? (You might need to look back over study 6 to refresh your memory.)

6. "The description of the excellent wife has as much to say to men as it does to women." What do you think?

7. How does the "excellent wife" make you feel?

8. Are there any areas of life where you would like to be more like the "excellent wife"? What can you do in order to make this happen?

9. What characteristics of the "excellent wife" do you see displayed in Jesus Christ?

 ## To finish

Have a look back over the previous studies. Have there been any lessons which you have found especially helpful? What made them helpful? With God's assistance, what changes are you going to make in your life as a result?

 ## Give thanks and pray

Thank our heavenly Father for promising that "If any of you lacks wisdom, let him ask God, who gives generously to all without reproach, and it will be given him" (Jas 1:5).

FOR THE LEADER

What are Pathway Bible Guides?

The Pathway Bible Guides aim to provide simple, straightforward Bible study material for:

- Christians who are new to studying the Bible (perhaps because they've been recently converted or because they have joined a Bible study group for the first time)
- Christians who find other studies[1] too much of a stretch.

Accordingly, we've designed the studies to be short, straightforward and easy to use, with a simple vocabulary. At the same time, we've tried to do justice to the passages being studied, and to model good Bible-reading principles. We've tried to be simple without being simplistic; no-nonsense without being no-content.

The questions and answers assume a small group context, but it should be easy to adapt them to suit different situations, such as individual study and one-to-one.

Your role as leader

Because many in your group may not be used to reading and discussing a Bible passage in a group context, a greater level of responsibility will fall to you as the leader of the discussions. There are the usual responsibilities of preparation, prayer and managing group dynamics. Then, in addition, there will be an extra dimension of forming and encouraging good Bible reading habits in people who may not have much of an idea of what those habits look like.

Questions have been kept deliberately brief and simple. For that reason, you may have to fill in some of the gaps that may have been addressed in, say, an Interactive Bible Study. Such 'filling in' may take the form of asking follow-up questions, or using your best judgement to work out when you might need to supply background information. That sort of information, and some suggestions about other questions you could ask, may be found in the following leader's notes. In addition, a *New Bible Dictionary* is always a useful aid to preparation, and simple commentaries such as those in the *Tyndale* or *Bible Speaks Today* series are often helpful. Consult them after you have done your own preparation.

On the question of background information, these studies are written from the assumption that God's word stands alone. God works through his Holy Spirit and the leaders he has gifted—such as you—to make his meaning clear. Assuming this to be true, the best interpreter and provider of background information for Scripture will not be academic historical research, but Scripture itself. Extra historical information may be useful for the purpose of illustration, but it is unnecessary for understanding and applying what God says to us.

The format of the studies

The discussion questions on each passage follow a simple pattern. There is a question at the beginning of each discussion that is intended to get people talking around the issues raised by the passage, and to give you some idea of how people are thinking. If the group turns out to be confident, motivated and comfortable with each other and the task at hand, you may even decide to skip this question. Alternatively, if the group members are shy or quiet, you may decide to think of related types of questions that you could add in to the study, so as to maintain momentum in a non-threatening way.

After the first question, the remaining questions work through the passage sequentially, alternating between observation, interpretation and application in a way that will become obvious when you do your own preparation. The final question of each discussion, just before the opportunity for prayer, could be used in some groups to encourage (say) one person each week to give a short talk (it could be 1 minute or 5 minutes, depending on the topic, and the people). The thinking here is that there's no better way to encourage understanding of a passage than to get people to the point where they can explain it to others. Use your judgement in making the best use of this final exercise each week, depending on the people in your group.

In an average group, it should be possible to work through the study in approximately 45 minutes. But it's important that you work out what your group is capable of given the time available, and make adjustments accordingly. Work out in advance which questions or sub-points can be omitted if time is short. And have a few supplementary questions or discussion starters up your sleeve if your group is dealing with the material quite quickly and hungering for more. Each group is different. It's your job as leader to use the printed material as 'Bible

Guides', and not as a set of questions that you must rigidly stick to regardless of your circumstances.

Preparation: 60/40/20

Ideally, group members should spend half an hour reading over the passage and pencilling in some answers *before* they come to the group. Not every group member will do this, of course, but encourage them with the idea that the more they prepare for the study, the more they will get out of the discussion.

In terms of your own preparation as leader, we recommend you put aside approximately *two hours*, either all at once or in two one-hour blocks, and that you divide up the time as follows:

- 60 minutes reading the passage and answering the questions yourself as best you can (without looking at the leader's notes or Bible commentaries).

- 40 minutes consulting the leader's notes (plus other resources, like commentaries). Add to your own answers, and jot down supplementary questions or other information that you want to have available as you lead the discussion. Make sure you write everything you need on the study pages—the last thing you want to do is to keep turning to the 'answers' in the back during the group discussion.

- 20 minutes praying about the study and for your group members.

This 60/40/20 pattern will help you to focus on the Bible, and what it's saying, rather than simply regurgitating to the group what is in the leader's notes. Remember these notes are just that—notes to offer some help and guidance. They are not the Bible! As a pattern of preparation, 60/40/20 also helps you to keep praying for yourself and your group, that God would give spiritual growth as his word is sown in your hearts (see Luke 8:4-15; 1 Cor 3:5-7).

If, for some reason, you have less or more time to spend in preparation, simply apply the 60/40/20 proportions accordingly.

---

1. Such as the Interactive Bible Study (IBS) series also available from Matthias Media.

1. THE GAINING OF WISDOM

Proverbs 1:1-6

▶ Remember 60/40/20

 ## Getting started

Stroll into any bookstore and you'll discover shelves full of self-help books—books with titles like *Secrets for Success and Happiness*, *The 10 Natural Laws of Successful Time and Life Management*, *More Than 60 Ways to Make Your Life Amazing* and *Your Best Year Yet*. Clearly many of us want help in negotiating life. We have lingering doubts we're not the best we can be. The 'Getting started' question taps into this search for self-improvement by gathering examples of the types of advice which have helped us improve our lives. This provides a good link into the book of Proverbs for, as we shall see in this study, the self-proclaimed aim of Proverbs is to help us live well.

Studying the passage

Proverbs is one of those very handy parts of the Bible which begins by telling us why it was written. Its purpose is described in verses 2-4:

> To know wisdom and instruction,
>   to understand words of insight,
> to receive instruction in wise dealing,
>   in righteousness, justice, and equity;
> to give prudence to the simple,
>   knowledge and discretion to the youth...

This purpose statement contains three noteworthy words: 'wisdom', 'prudence' and 'discretion'. Each word provides a helpful insight into the value and purpose of the book (question 2). In the Bible, 'wisdom' is practical knowledge. Wisdom is more than knowing facts; wisdom is making the right use of facts. Wisdom is knowing what to do next in life. The word 'prudence' carries with it the idea of exercising care and good judgement in planning for the future. Prudence is being able to make *present* decisions so as to best achieve *future* goals. The word 'discretion' brings with it overtones of self-restraint and sensitivity: the discreet person makes right decisions in such a way as to not cause offence or hurt to others.

Proverbs, therefore, offers its readers rich instruction in the art of living—instruction that enables us to live stable, good, coherent and effective lives. For this reason, Proverbs is an incredibly useful book for our restless, modern society where so many of us struggle to know how to get the best out of life. Ironically, though, Proverb's emphasis on prudence, discipline and self-restraint is not a message many want to hear nowadays (question 3).

As well as describing the purpose of the book, the opening verses also inform us of the pattern of the book. In particular we discover that the book contains a range of sayings (v. 6; question 5). This range will include proverbs (the one-sentence life insights for which the book is most famous), sayings (described as 'parables' in the NIV—stories or sayings, often with a biting or satirical edge to them, from which a life lesson can be drawn) and riddles (sayings from which a lesson is not immediately obvious). Proverbs is therefore a book which will require thoughtful reading. It is not simply a list of universal rules which will guarantee us successful lives. As we will discover, the book is more subtle and multilayered than that (see study 5 if you can't wait).

As well as explaining the purpose and pattern of the book, the opening verses also introduce us to a very significant person associated with the book. According to verse 1, this is a book closely connected with King Solomon, the king of Israel and son of King David (question 6). This is not surprising since, within the Old Testament, Solomon appears as a great patron and sponsor of wisdom. 1 Kings 4:29 informs us that "God gave Solomon wisdom and understanding beyond measure, and breadth of mind like the sand on the seashore". Solomon spoke 3,000 proverbs, described plant life, and taught about animals, birds, reptiles and fish (1 Kgs 4:32-33). Solomon was therefore an excellent instructor in the art of living (question 7).

What is perhaps most significant is that the mention of Solomon in verse 1 further strengthens the tight association between wisdom and God's king in the Bible. Tragically, this association was soon tainted by a long line of foolish and immoral kings who came after Solomon. However, the Old Testament never completely loses this connection between God's king and wisdom; instead, it holds it out as an ideal. This is most clearly seen in the prophets, where God's coming Christ is linked with wisdom and understanding (question 8)—for example, in Isaiah 11:2:

> And the Spirit of the LORD shall rest upon him,
>> the Spirit of wisdom and understanding,
>> the Spirit of counsel and might,
>> the Spirit of knowledge and the fear of the LORD.

Given this link between wisdom and God's king, it is therefore, no surprise that when Jesus Christ appears the New Testament, writers portray him as the bearer of great wisdom:

> The queen of the South will rise up at the judgment with this generation and condemn it, for she came from the ends of the earth to hear the wisdom of Solomon, and behold, something greater than Solomon is here. (Matt 12:42)

These links between wisdom, God's king and Jesus Christ carry enormous implications for how we are to live our lives. They help us see that obeying Jesus will lead to us getting the most out of life. If Solomon's wisdom and understanding were "beyond measure, and breadth of mind like the sand on the seashore", how much more is Jesus' wisdom and understanding! Insight and discernment can be found in his every word.

As children of God saved by Christ's death and resurrection it is therefore our privilege and blessing to do what Jesus says, for his wisdom is beyond question. Jesus Christ knows better than anyone else how we can be the best people we can be. So, irrespective, of what our friends or family or even our own desires might urge us to do, we must always say "Yes!" to Jesus Christ, for someone even greater than Solomon has come (question 9).

To finish

The finishing question is designed to help us reflect on the confidence we have in Jesus as the giver of true wisdom. It's important to linger on this truth because, to the ears of the world, much of what Jesus says sounds foolish. Jesus' teachings on self-restraint, servanthood and the priorities of the kingdom are stunningly counter-cultural. The opening verses of Proverbs are therefore of great benefit in helping us appreciate God's Christ as the wisest man of all. In his words we can have full confidence.

2. THE BEGINNING OF WISDOM

· ·

Proverbs 1:7

▶ Remember 60/40/20

 Getting started

Of all the valuable truths offered in the book of Proverbs, there is one truth which towers over every other. Of all the precious gems embedded in the book, there is one mother lode. It is the lesson that we must fear God.

But what exactly does it mean to fear God? What sort of relationship does this describe? This study investigates these critical issues. The 'Getting started' question is designed to introduce the topic by encouraging discussion about the ways in which we fail to fear God enough.

Studying the passage

It is significant that, having explained the purpose of the book in verses 1-6 (see previous study), the very first lesson which Proverbs offers is "The fear of the LORD is the beginning of knowledge" (Prov 1:7).

This is the first lesson offered because it is *the* foundational lesson upon which everything else is based. For this reason, questions 1-5 all focus on what is being taught in this one verse.

Fearing God means to be in reverent, humble awe before his power and majesty (question 1). So fearing God is a much more positive idea than simply being 'scared' or 'frightened' of God. When we use the latter phrase, we tend to think of someone or something which is unpredictable and which, at any time, might lash out and harm us without reason. That is not the case with God at all. The Scriptures comfort us with the thought that God is rich in mercy and love, and therefore he is someone in whom we can take refuge (question 2).

However, the goodness of God doesn't negate the importance of knowing our rightful place before him. God's power and holiness is beyond our wildest dreams. He created everything with just a word, and he can destroy whole nations with ease. He is able to punish horribly those who ignore and rebel against him (question 3). This truth must always affect the way we respond to him. Yes, God is wonderfully gracious, but we must never presume on his goodness. The idea of defying God should fill us with complete dread. The idea of disobeying God should utterly terrify us. If it doesn't, we have no idea who we're dealing with!

In verse 7, the phrase "the beginning of knowledge" is also significant. It highlights the manner in which the fear of the Lord is both the starting point and the foundational truth upon which *all* wisdom always depends. The fear of the Lord is like the foundation of a building: it's the first thing that's laid down, and it continues to be important to the stability of that building throughout the life of that building. In the same way, the fear of the Lord never stops being important to the stability of our lives (question 4).

Verse 7 is therefore a critically important lesson to live out. If we aren't prepared to stand in reverent awe of the one who designed the world we're living in, and if that awe doesn't shape the way we live, our lives will eventually crack and fall down. No matter how smart we are—no matter how impressive our expertise—if there's no "fear of the LORD", ultimately there's no real wisdom!

The importance of fearing the Lord is not only reflected in the fact that it is the first lesson given in the book, it is also reflected in the fact that it's an often-repeated lesson (see, for example, Proverbs 2:5, 3:7, 8:13, 9:10, 14:27, 15:16, 15:33, 16:6, 19:23, 22:4, 23:17, 24:21; question 6). These verses emphasize that the consequence of fearing God is a stable and blessed life. This is good for us to appreciate because a word like 'fear' can arouse in us negative feelings of dread. Proverbs, however, is clear: the "fear of the LORD" is not something to avoid but rather the starting point for a joyous, fulfilling life.

It's important to note that when Proverbs urges us to fear God, the author of Proverbs means specifically Yahweh, the God of Israel (see the note in question 7). Here Proverbs parts company with the prevailing thought of our modern politically correct society: whereas our world promotes the idea that belief in *any* god is acceptable, Proverbs promotes the truth that there is only *one* God (question 7). Fear of *him* is the foundation on which we build our lives.

When we step out of Proverbs and survey the broader biblical landscape, we discover that the fear of the Lord is also extended to the fear of his chosen king. An excellent example of this can be found in Psalm 2 (question 8). In this psalm, the enemies of God are gathered against God and his king. However, their opposition is pathetic: the Anointed One is able to smash the enemies of God as if they were pottery (Ps 2:9). Therefore the psalmist concludes,

> Now therefore, O kings, be wise;
> > be warned, O rulers of the earth.
> Serve the LORD with fear,
> > and rejoice with trembling.
> Kiss the Son,
> > lest he be angry, and you perish in the way,
> > for his wrath is quickly kindled.
> Blessed are all who take refuge in him. (Ps 2:10-12)

It is no surprise, then, that the New Testament consistently urges us to live in the fear of King Jesus, the Anointed One of God (question 9). For the Christian, this means living a lifestyle of humble, reverent obedience in every aspect of day-to-day existence. But it also means a life of blessing, security, deep joy and surpassing hope, for if Jesus is for us, who can be against us (Rom 8:31)?

> The fear of the LORD leads to life,
> > and whoever has it rests satisfied;
> > he will not be visited by harm. (Prov 19:23)

 ## To finish

Fearing Jesus rightly is not always easy. We can often be intimidated by the powers and authorities of this world. The final question is designed to stimulate helpful sharing about practical ways in which we can encourage one another to fear the Lord by retaining a clear focus on Jesus our master.

3. THE VOICE OF WISDOM

Proverbs 9

▶ Remember 60/40/20

 ## Getting started

Every day we are bombarded by different voices telling us how to live our lives. These voices come from an endless number of sources—family, friends, work colleagues, professionals, advertisements, and so on. The 'Getting started' question raises the issue of which voices might be better to listen to. This question is raised because Proverbs 9 summarizes all the voices down to two: the voice of Wisdom and the voice of Folly. Proverbs does this to demonstrate that only one of those voices is ever worth taking notice of: the voice of Wisdom.

Studying the passage

In this study, it may seem a little strange to jump ahead to chapter 9. However, within the book of Proverbs, chapter 9 serves as a summary of 1:8-9:18. An understanding of chapter 9 will therefore provide us with a good framework with which to go back and examine some of the earlier chapters. We will do this in our next study.

Proverbs 9 opens with a vivid word picture of wisdom, personified as a woman who has prepared a banquet (question 1). She invites all who wish to come to feast with her, and encourages all to come and live life to the full—to live a life of understanding and meaning (v. 6; question 2). The fullness of this life is signified by the seven pillars of the house, for in the Bible seven often symbolizes fullness and completeness.

Central to Wisdom's invitation is the advice that "The fear of the LORD is the beginning of wisdom, and the knowledge of the Holy One is insight" (v. 10). This comes as no surprise, given what we discovered in our last study: the reverent fear of the Lord is the foundational truth upon which the wise life must be built. Only by knowing our place before the Giver of Life can we make the most of our own lives (question 3). For this reason, the consequences of following Wisdom are understanding and life. Her banquet is a rich and varied feast—a feast which provides the simple (i.e. the naïve and untaught) with fullness of life (question 4):

> Leave your simple ways, and live,
> and walk in the way of insight...
>
> For by me your days will be multiplied,
> and years will be added to your life.
> If you are wise, you are wise for yourself;
> if you scoff, you alone will bear it. (Prov 9:6, 11-12)

By showing us the balance and blessing which come from accepting Wisdom's invitation, Proverbs 9 provides a suitable summary for much of the earlier chapters. For example, consider the voice of Wisdom in Proverbs 8:

> By me kings reign,
> and rulers decree what is just;
> by me princes rule,
> and nobles, all who govern justly.
> I love those who love me,
> and those who seek me diligently find me.
> Riches and honour are with me,
> enduring wealth and righteousness...
>
> Blessed is the one who listens to me,
> watching daily at my gates,
> waiting beside my doors.
> For whoever finds me finds life
> and obtains favour from the LORD... (Prov 8:15-18, 34-35)

Wisdom, however, is not alone in Proverbs 9. A competing voice is raised: the voice of Folly. Folly is personified as another woman, inviting guests to *her* house and *her* banquet. Indeed, Folly's invitation is identical to that of Wisdom's (compare verse 4 to verse 16). The similarities between Wisdom and Folly highlight the deceitfulness of the latter. Like Wisdom, Folly can seem so reasonable and appealing at the time. Like Wisdom, Folly seems to promise so much (questions 5-6).

But, despite outward appearances, Folly does not humbly fear the Lord. We are told in verse 13 that she is loud and knows nothing. Verse 17 points out that, in contrast to the food and drink which Wisdom herself has mixed (v. 5), the food and drink of Folly is stolen and secretive. Folly lures us into a life of ill-gotten gains and blessings obtained through disobedience. In essence, Folly tempts us to live in mockery of God rather than in fear of God (question 7). For this reason, the consequences of following Folly are the exact opposite to that of Wisdom: Wisdom brings life and understanding; Folly brings despair and emptiness (question 8):

> But he does not know that the dead are there,
>> that her guests are in the depths of Sheol. (Prov 9:18)

By painting this vivid picture of Wisdom and Folly with words, Proverbs provides us with a very insightful and valuable life lesson: our choices in life often come down to a simple decision between Wisdom and Folly—a choice between acting out of fear of the Lord, or acting in a way which ignores the Lord. In this respect, Jesus' choices at the time of his temptation in the wilderness are a helpful example to follow. In Matthew 4, Jesus is tempted with sweet rewards— no less than the splendour of all the kingdoms of the world! However, Jesus saw through the deceitfulness of these temptations, and rejected folly, choosing instead to live in submission and obedience to his heavenly Father. In so doing, Jesus again stands as the great wise man of the Scriptures (question 10).

To finish

Folly often tempts us with short-term worldly gains and experiences at the expense of long-term spiritual blessings. The finishing question asks us to consider the ways in which we can keep our focus on spiritual and eternal matters. Hebrews 12:1-3 may prove to be a helpful passage to ponder in your group:

> Therefore, since we are surrounded by so great a cloud of witnesses, let us also lay aside every weight, and sin which clings so closely, and let us run with endurance the race that is set before us, looking to Jesus, the founder and perfecter of our faith, who for the joy that was set before him endured the cross, despising the shame, and is seated at the right hand of the throne of God.
> Consider him who endured from sinners such hostility against himself, so that you may not grow weary or fainthearted.

4. THE OPPOSITE OF WISDOM

Proverbs 1-8

▶ Remember 60/40/20

 Getting started

In many ways, the 'Getting started' question for this study reiterates a question that has already been asked on several occasions: how do you live in the fear of the Lord? It gives you another opportunity to discuss the challenges involved in living in the fear of the Lord. Repeating this theme highlights the importance of the lesson: the fear of the Lord is *the* lesson we must learn if we are to appreciate the wisdom that comes from Proverbs. The fear of the Lord is also relevant to several questions within this study (see the comments below for questions 2, 5 and 8).

In our last study, we discovered from Proverbs 9 that folly (i.e. *not* living in the fear of the Lord) tantalizes us with the prospect of sweet rewards. Despite outward appearances, however, the consequences of choosing folly are dark indeed. Folly leads to death, the grave and the judgement of God. This means it's vital for us to be able to recognize and avoid the voice of folly. Proverbs 1-8 very helpfully provides us with examples of some of the disguises folly can wear. In those chapters, we meet some of the voices which folly might take on in order to deceive us. In this study, we look at three such voices in particular: the voice of the sinner, the voice of the adulteress and the voice of the sluggard.

Studying the passage

Please note that the same three questions are repeated in each section of the study. (They do say that repetition is an important tool in learning!) This has been done in order to stress the fact that beneath all three voices is the one voice: the voice of folly. This voice tempts us to live in disobedience to the Lord, not in the fear of the Lord. It promises us rewards but only delivers death.

The voice of the sinner

In Proverbs 1:10-19 we meet the voice of the sinner. This voice entices us with the prospect of easy gain through violence (question 1):

> ..."Come with us, let us lie in wait for blood;
>> let us ambush the innocent without reason;
> like Sheol let us swallow them alive,
>> and whole, like those who go down to the pit;
> we shall find all precious goods,
>> we shall fill our houses with plunder;
> throw in your lot among us;
>> we will all have one purse"... (Prov 1:11-14)

However, selfishness and violence betray a failure to live in the fear of the Lord. The consequence of such ill-gotten gain is destruction (vv. 18-19; question 2). The voice of the sinner is, therefore, nothing less than the voice of folly in disguise.

Question 3 may at first seem to be a difficult question to answer since relatively few people have been physically attacked and robbed by someone. However, it is helpful to think through the different ways that violence and selfishness might express themselves in our lives.

The lesson here is a good one to master: the voices of aggression, greed and selfish bullying are never worth listening to, even if they do offer short-term gain (question 3).

The voice of the adulteress

In Proverbs 5 we meet the voice of the adulteress. This voice entices us with the prospect of pleasure and sexual satisfaction (question 4):

> For the lips of a forbidden woman drip honey,
>> and her speech is smoother than oil... (Prov 5:3)

However, unfaithfulness and adultery betray a failure to live in the fear of the Lord. The consequence of such pleasure-seeking is destruction (vv. 4-6, 11-14, 22-23; question 5). The voice of the adulteress is, therefore, nothing less than the voice of folly in disguise: both lead to Sheol (compare 5:5 with 9:18).

The lesson here is a good one to master: the voices of pornography, sexual immorality, immodest fashion and inappropriate flirting are never worth listening to, even if they do offer short-term excitement and pleasure (question 6).

The voice of the sluggard

In Proverbs 6:6-11, we meet the voice of the sluggard. This voice entices us with the prospect of rest and relaxation (question 7):

> A little sleep, a little slumber,
> a little folding of the hands to rest… (Prov 6:10)

However, self-absorbed laziness betrays a failure to live in the fear of the Lord. The consequences of such laziness are poverty and ruin (v. 11; question 8). The voice of the sluggard is, therefore, nothing less than the voice of folly in disguise. With biting sarcasm, Proverbs points out that even the ant recognizes this (v. 6-8)!

The lesson here is a good one to master: the voices of laziness, idleness and negligence are never worth listening to, even if they do offer short-term comfort (question 9).

To finish

Hopefully the repetition of questions within this study has reinforced a valuable lesson: the voice of folly can come to us under many different guises. Therefore, we must be alert when making life choices. The final question urges us to consider what other voices folly may take. Examples of these include: the voice of the gossip, the voice of the slanderer, the voice of the proud, the voice of the liar, the voice of the wicked, the voice of the vulgar, the voice of the ungrateful, the voice of the unforgiving and the voice of the greedy. Behind each of these the wise person can discern the voice of folly.

To reinforce the lesson of this study it may be helpful to close by reading Ephesians 4:20-5:7 together. This passage was not included in the study due to time constraints, but it raises many of the issues of this study in the context of putting off our former way of life and putting on "the new self, created after the likeness of God in true righteousness and holiness" (Eph 4:24).

5. THE PATTERNS OF WISDOM

Proverbs 16

▶ Remember 60/40/20

 Getting started

Life can be chaotic. Sometimes it can seem *so* chaotic, it can be unfathomable and overwhelming. Things can happen to us for no apparent rhyme or reason, and we are left not knowing what to do or how to cope. The opening question encourages people to discuss this perception of life because the large central section of Proverbs 10-29 reassures us with the news that life *does* have order and therefore it *can* be managed. Indeed, despite the complexity of life, it can actually be managed *well*.

Studying the passage

The opening four questions investigate the manner in which Proverbs presents its material. This is important because a common approach to Proverbs is to dissect and categorize the book by gathering together all the different verses which relate to a common theme. This approach can be helpful, and the next study will in fact do this, however it is significant that Proverbs itself does not present its lessons in this way.

In this study, Proverbs 16 is treated as a representative chapter of the entire section of chapters 10-29. The chapter reflects the way that Proverbs throws together many sayings in no obvious order. Certainly some topics frequently recur (in the next study we'll look at some of the more common themes). However, it is difficult to discern any strict order or logic in the way the topics are arranged (questions 2-3). By presenting its material in this way, Proverbs mimics the very nature of life: life brings with it recurring responsibilities and choices, but often with no obvious order or pattern to them.

But despite the apparent lack of order in its material, Proverbs still manages to convey the impression that life is not completely chaotic. It does this by repeatedly reinforcing two main principles which flow out of life. These principles can be thought of as:

1. Truths based on God's character

Many sayings in Proverbs flow directly from the fear of the Lord—from who God is and his righteousness. These are things that we *must* do out of reverent obedience. In these sayings, certain types of behaviour are declared to be good (i.e. what God delights in) and other types of behaviour are declared to be bad (i.e. they make God angry). Often these sayings refer to what the righteous and wise person does as opposed to what the sinner or fool does. In chapter 16, examples of these sayings include:

Everyone who is arrogant in heart is an abomination to the LORD;
be assured, he will not go unpunished. (v. 5)

By steadfast love and faithfulness iniquity is atoned for,
and by the fear of the LORD one turns away from evil. (v. 6)

Better is a little with righteousness
than great revenues with injustice. (v. 8)

It is an abomination to kings to do evil,
for the throne is established by righteousness. (v. 12)

How much better to get wisdom than gold!
To get understanding is to be chosen rather than silver. (v. 16)

Whoever is slow to anger is better than the mighty,
and he who rules his spirit than he who takes a city. (v. 32)

Even though there are a lot of different topics covered in these proverbs, they are all linked in that they pronounce judgement that something is good or something is bad: one will be punished by God while the other will be rewarded. These proverbs concern issues of right and wrong. If we truly fear the Lord, these are not matters of opinion but obligations: these are the sorts of ways that we *must* live (question 5).

2. Truths that come from observing God's world

Proverbs provides many other sayings which are simple observations about life. These observations describe the way things usually are without making any real value judgements about them. Examples of these in chapter 16 include:

> In the light of a king's face there is life,
> > and his favour is like the clouds that bring the spring rain. (v. 15)

> Pride goes before destruction,
> > and a haughty spirit before a fall. (v. 18)

> A worker's appetite works for him;
> > his mouth urges him on. (v. 26)

> Whoever winks his eyes plans dishonest things;
> > he who purses his lips brings evil to pass. (v. 30)

These sayings are generalizations about life in this world. They don't always reflect on whether what they describe is good or bad. For example, verse 18 simply observes that pride will often precede a fall. Although we know from other parts of Scripture that pride is wrong, verse 18 does not state this.

It's also important to note that these observations about life describe what *often* happens but not what *always* happens. They are generalizations, not absolute rules. Sometimes pride *doesn't* go before a fall. Sometimes a wink of the eye *doesn't* necessarily imply dishonesty.

Nevertheless, these are practical and helpful reflections on what is the usual pattern of things in God's world (question 6). Proverbs gives them to us so that we can reflect on them, and learn to live wisely and well as a result. "This is how things are in God's world", says Proverbs. "So pause and think carefully: How will this guide your behaviour in different circumstances?"

It can be difficult sometimes to determine whether a saying in Proverbs is an 'obligation' or an 'observation' (question 7). Some people find this a little disconcerting. However, it's helpful to remember that Proverbs *wants* us to think carefully about its sayings (Prov 1:4-6). Proverbs makes this quite explicit at several points—for example, Proverbs 26:4-5 where we read the following advice:

> Answer not a fool according to his folly,
> > lest you be like him yourself.

> Answer a fool according to his folly,
>   lest he be wise in his own eyes.

In the space of two verses the exact opposite advice is given! This has been done deliberately, because true wisdom does not come from simply knowing a long string of proverbs; true wisdom is knowing *when to apply the proverb rightly*. Again, as Proverbs points out,

> Like a thorn that goes up into the hand of a drunkard
>   is a proverb in the mouth of fools. (Prov 26:9)

The obligations and observations of life contained in Proverbs 10-29 reflect the fact that this world is not completely chaotic. There are regularities and patterns in life. Proverbs shows us this to teach us that life *can* be managed.

In addition, Proverbs highlighting the fact that life has order and regularity has the effect of pointing us to Christ. Christ is the maker and sustainer of the world, as well as the one to whom all creation must conform and submit (Eph 1:9-10, Col 1:16-17; question 8). Therefore life will only ever make complete sense when it is lived under the Lordship of Christ. This is what the Bible means when it says that Christ holds "all the treasures of wisdom and knowledge" (Col 2:3).

To finish

In this study we have discovered that Proverbs reassures us with the news that despite the chaotic nature of life, there is still order. Regularities and relationships are observable. There is pattern and reason to the created order— a pattern that is best understood in Christ.

These are great truths, yet the rough and tumble of life can, at times, hide these truths from us. In the midst of disappointment, frustration, anxiety or pain, life can truly seem out of control. The last question prompts us to consider these times so that when they occur, we don't lose sight of the comforting truths of this study.

6. THE LESSONS OF WISDOM

Proverbs 10-29

▶ Remember 60/40/20

 Getting started

In this study, we dive headlong into the sea of short, pithy sayings which comprise the bulk of the central chapters of Proverbs. The 'Getting started' question is intended to be a light-hearted but helpful introduction to the study, encouraging members to share modern-day proverbs which they already know and which may have proven helpful in their own lives. There are many to choose from: "Too many cooks spoil the broth", "A bird in the hand is worth two in the bush", "Don't count your chickens before they hatch", and so on. When it comes to Proverbs, then, we are on familiar ground; we all know catchy sayings containing wise advice. However, the sayings of Proverbs come with even more power for they are no less than the wise advice of God himself!

Studying the passage

In our previous study, we discovered that the large middle section of Proverbs (chapters 10-29) provides us with many obligations derived from God's character and observations about how to best live life. In this study, we dip further into these chapters by investigating what specific wisdom they offer on three important areas of life: wealth, words and work. There are a lot of verses to read here, so if you are working in a large group, it might be helpful to divide into three smaller groups, take one topic each, and then report back at the end.

Wealth

Proverbs has a lot to say about money and wealth. On the topic of how we are to earn it (question 1), Proverbs makes clear that any form of injustice or wickedness is disapproved of by God (e.g. 28:20-22). Along with this obligation, Proverbs also provides numerous observations about how wealth is best obtained in a measured and thoughtful manner. Rash decisions, hastiness in seeking to make money and 'get-rich-quick' schemes more often than not end in ruin (e.g. 12:11, 13:11).

Proverbs is not just concerned with how we *earn* money, but also how we *spend* it (question 2). On this topic, the repeated lesson is that God will honour and bless those who are generous to others in their use of money:

> Whoever is generous to the poor lends to the LORD,
>   and he will repay him for his deed. (Prov 19:17)

The above lessons about how to gain and use wealth flow from the deeper lesson that righteousness is far more important than gold or silver. God is far more interested in us—our fear of him—than our bank balance (question 3):

> Riches do not profit in the day of wrath,
>   but righteousness delivers from death. (Prov 11:4)

Words

As with wealth, Proverbs has a great deal to say about our speech. Proverbs recognizes that our words are incredibly powerful (question 4). Our words can do enormous damage as well as bring wonderful comfort. The saying "Sticks and stones will break my bones but words will never hurt me" is one you will definitely not find in Proverbs. On the contrary, how we speak to each other matters enormously.

Because of the power of our words, Proverbs encourages us to think carefully about what we say *before* we say it (10:19), and to strive for gracious, gentle and appropriate words (question 5). Alternatively, dishonest, selfish and insulting speech is to be avoided at all costs. Not only does such speech reflect a failure to fear the Lord, it also leads to calamity and ruin (e.g. 16:28, 26:28; question 6).

Work

Work is one of those areas of life where it's really hard to get the balance right. Proverbs provides wise insights, starting with the observation that work in itself is a good and helpful activity. However, Proverbs has no word of encouragement for the sluggard; they will reap what they sow—that is, nothing (question 7)! We first discovered this lesson back in study 4 when we were introduced to the voice of the sluggard:

> A little sleep, a little slumber,
> a little folding of the hands to rest,
> and poverty will come upon you like a robber,
> and want like an armed man. (Prov 6:10-11)

The diligent worker, however, will have security and food. This is an observation which rings true of so much in life (question 8).

When it comes to work, Proverbs is more concerned with the *way* in which we are to work rather than the *type* of work we do (question 9). As with all areas of life, work needs to be done in the fear of the Lord. This means we are to do things in a just and honest manner. Integrity and righteousness must always be ideals to strive for. This is a helpful corrective for the workaholic, career-driven ones among us. The way in which we pursue our jobs must never be used to justify or undermine the way in which we care for and support others—especially those in our own families.

To finish

The lessons of Proverbs are reinforced for the Christian in several ways. As in all of life, our attitudes to wealth (2 Cor 8:7-9), words (Eph 4:29-30) and work (Eph 6:5-8) are transformed by our desire to please Jesus Christ. Therefore, we seek to put off our old self and "put on the new self, created after the likeness of God in true righteousness and holiness" (Eph 4:24). Furthermore, we also live by the Spirit, who leads us to put to death the misdeeds of the sinful nature (Gal 5:16-25).

7. THE SEARCH FOR WISDOM

Proverbs 30

▶ Remember 60/40/20

 ## Getting started

One of the strongest—if not *the* strongest—lesson of Proverbs has been that the fear of the Lord is the beginning of wisdom. Only when we know the one true Creator can we start to make the best sense of his creation. In this study, we will examine a case study where this truth is realized in the life of an individual. The 'Getting started' question introduces the issues that are at stake perhaps a little provocatively by asking whether or not Christians are wiser than other people. Some people might object to such a thought, pointing out that many non-Christians are extremely clever. This may provide a good opportunity for you to revise and clarify what is meant by 'wisdom' in Proverbs. In the Bible, wisdom is practical knowledge: wisdom is more than knowing facts, wisdom is making the right use of facts. Wisdom is knowing how to best negotiate life (see study 1).

Studying the passage

In Proverbs 30, we are introduced to a person identified as Agur son of Jakeh. Agur is a man searching for wisdom and meaning in life (vv. 1-3; question 1).

Possibly the best translation of verse 1 is the one mentioned in the footnotes of the ESV (and NIV). In other words, Agur is "of Massa", an Ishmaelite clan (cf. Gen 25:14). There are several reasons why this translation should be favoured:

1. The use of the word 'oracle' here is quite unusual. 'Oracle' is a word that is generally associated with prophets. For it to appear in a book of wisdom literature like Proverbs is highly unconventional.

2. Translating it as 'Massa' would also make more sense of Proverbs 31:1 where the same word appears. This verse mentions King Lemuel, however no king by that name is ever recorded in Israel's history. This would not be surprising if, in fact, Lemuel is an Ishmaelite king.

3. If Agur is, in fact, a Gentile searching for wisdom, this explains his statements in verses 2-3. As a Gentile, Agur would have lived without the benefit of God's revelation to Israel. The apostle Paul describes the Old Testament Gentile as being far from God—"alienated from the commonwealth of Israel and strangers to the covenants of promise, having no hope and without God in the world" (Eph 2:11-12; question 2).

In his search for wisdom, Agur realizes that he must have a competent and experienced teacher, and that the Maker of the world would be the best qualified (v. 4). At the very least, his teacher would need to be someone very close to the Maker of the world—perhaps even his son. The question, however, is, "Who could that be?" Who has established the end of the earth? Who has gone up to heaven and come down again? What is his name or the name of his son? "Tell me if you know", Agur pleads (question 3).

For the Christian, the solution to Agur's plea is obvious: Jesus Christ is the Son of God who has come down from heaven and who has established the ends of the earth (question 4). Agur, however, is a Gentile, living on the other side of the cross to us. Yet God is good; Agur does, in fact, find wisdom in the word of God:

> Every word of God proves true;
>> he is a shield to those who take refuge in him.
> Do not add to his words,
>> lest he rebuke you and you be found a liar. (Prov 30:5-6)

The interesting thing about these verses is that verse 5 is a quote from Psalm 18:30 and verse 6 is a very strong echo of Deuteronomy 4:2. In other words, Agur's search for wisdom has brought him to the Old Testament, God's words to Israel (question 6). To put it another way, in the Scriptures of the Old Testament Agur discovers the fear of the Lord. Agur's fear of the Lord is reflected in verses 7-9:

Two things I ask of you;
        deny them not to me before I die:
Remove far from me falsehood and lying;
        give me neither poverty nor riches;
feed me with the food that is needful for me,
        lest I be full and deny you
and say, "Who is the LORD?"
        or lest I be poor and steal
and profane the name of my God.

With these words, Agur describes the importance of knowing the God of Israel. Since the fear of the Lord is the beginning of wisdom, to disown or dishonour him is foolishness beyond belief. This is why Agur is an excellent case study, illustrating how true wisdom in this life can only come from the one true God (question 7).

In the rest of the chapter, Agur offers different insights he has gained after having come to see that the word of God is true. It's a challenging section because some of the lessons seem obscure, however the basic pattern of the text is that Agur makes a statement which he then illustrates with four examples from the world. For example, verse 10 offers comment about the dangers of a hateful tongue. Verses 11-14 then follow with four examples of other hateful things: people who curse their parents (v. 11), those who love themselves and so hate others (v. 12), those who give hateful and arrogant looks (v. 13) and finally, those who hate the needy by taking advantage of them (v. 14; question 8).

In these lessons, Agur repeats some of the themes found earlier in the book—for example, the importance of our speech (v. 10), concern for the needy (v. 14) and the danger of the adulteress (v. 20; question 9).

 ## To finish

Proverbs 30 provides us with a wonderful case study of a person who has only been able to make sense of life by coming to know the true and living God. The finishing question is designed to help personalize Agur's journey to wisdom. Use this question as an opportunity to allow people to share how being a follower of Jesus has helped them make better sense of life.

8. LADY WISDOM

Proverbs 31:10-31

▶ Remember 60/40/20

 Getting started

The book of Proverbs concludes with a picture of domestic bliss—a description of an extraordinary wife of excellence. The passage is, in fact, a poem written in the form of an acrostic. Each line of these verses in Hebrew begins with the next letter of the Hebrew alphabet: the first word of verse 10 starts with the Hebrew equivalent of 'A', the first word of verse 11 starts with the Hebrew equivalent of 'B', and so on, all the way to verse 31 which begins with the Hebrew equivalent of 'Z'. This acrostic structure highlights that these final verses are a summary of everything that has gone before them: here at the end of the book, we quite literally have the A-Z of Proverbs.

This vivid description of an "excellent wife" forms an excellent summary of the whole of Proverbs. It is a tantalizing description of what life could be like if the reader were to live out the book's instructions. The 'Getting started' question is designed to encourage people to develop their own picture of what life would be like if we were to "put into practice all the lessons we've discovered so far in Proverbs". It might be interesting for your group to compare these descriptions to the wife of excellence as you progress through this study.

Studying the passage

Because the description of the "excellent wife" serves as a summary of the entire book, questions 1-5 are aimed at drawing the links between this passage and lessons from previous studies. For example, in study 1, we discovered that the book of Proverbs can help us live a wise, righteous and prudent life (1:2-4). All three qualities are exemplified in the "excellent wife": her wisdom is specifically mentioned (v. 26), her discretion is reflected in the way her right decisions cause no offence or hurt (v. 28), and her prudence is displayed in the confidence with which she faces the future (vv. 21, 25).

In study 2, we learned that the "fear of the LORD is the beginning of knowledge" (1:7). The "excellent wife" has based her life on this foundational truth (vv. 29-30).

In study 3, we saw wisdom described as a woman in Proverbs 9. There are a number of similarities between the descriptions in chapter 9 and the descriptions in chapter 31: in both chapters, the women provide ample food, they offer wise instruction, and they centre their lives on the fear of the Lord.

In study 4, we were given advice about the foolishness of the sinner, the adulteress and the sluggard. In chapter 31, the wife of excellence is the opposite of all of these. Instead of being violently selfish, she is gentle and kind in her generosity (v. 20). Instead of being sexually wayward, she is faithful and dedicated to her husband and family (vv. 11, 27-28). Instead of being a sluggard, she hardly ever sleeps but spends her time working industriously (vv. 15, 27).

In study 6, we were given life lessons about wealth, words and work. The wife of excellence exemplifies them all: she obtains wealth by hard work but is generous in her use of it (vv. 19-20), her words are wise and her teaching is kind (v. 26), and she is a diligent worker of integrity (vv. 24-25).

The "excellent wife" is indeed a vivid and exhaustive image of the key lessons of Proverbs. Unfortunately, however, Proverbs 31 is often a misunderstood and undervalued part of Proverbs. Some women read this section and get depressed and intimidated by the amazing competence and energy of the wife of excellence. Their feelings can, in turn, be compounded by selfish and uncaring husbands who use the passage to find fault with their wives. The end result is that the point of the chapter is completely missed, and the passage itself is criticized for being old-fashioned, out-of-date and sexist. These sorts of reactions fail to view the chapter in its context. The description of the excellent wife carries a lesson for *both* men and women because it serves as a description of what life could be like for anyone who lives out the lessons of the book (question 6).

On one level, you could read back through these verses and replace the "excellent wife" with 'wisdom'. Doing that makes it not just a chapter for Christian wives but a chapter for everyone. Whatever you do, marry wisdom. Hold it near and dear. Let it shape your life. Fear the Lord. Hold onto righteousness, kindness and truth. The description of the "excellent wife" is therefore meant to enthuse and motivate us (question 7).

In this respect, the wife of excellence, like all of Proverbs, points us again to Jesus Christ, the great man of wisdom. Her prudence, self-discipline, righteousness, wisdom, diligence and generous spirit can also be seen in Jesus Christ—and in a greater and more perfect way (question 9). Therefore, whatever you do, hold Jesus Christ near and dear. Let him shape your life.

 ## To finish

Being the final study in this series, now is a good time to review the lessons your group has learned along the way—especially those which have been particularly helpful to them.

Matthias Media is an evangelical publishing ministry that seeks to persuade all Christians of the truth of God's purposes in Jesus Christ as revealed in the Bible, and equip them with high-quality resources, so that by the work of the Holy Spirit they will:

- abandon their lives to the honour and service of Christ in daily holiness and decision-making
- pray constantly in Christ's name for the fruitfulness and growth of his gospel
- speak the Bible's life-changing word whenever and however they can—in the home, in the world and in the fellowship of his people.

Our resources range from Bible studies and books through to training courses, audio sermons and children's Sunday School material. To find out more, and to access samples and free downloads, visit our website:

www.matthiasmedia.com

How to buy our resources

1. Direct from us over the internet:
   – in the US: www.matthiasmedia.com
   – in Australia: www.matthiasmedia.com.au

2. Direct from us by phone: please visit our website for current phone contact information.

3. Through a range of outlets in various parts of the world. Visit **www.matthiasmedia.com/contact** for details about recommended retailers in your part of the world.

4. Trade enquiries can be addressed to:
   – in the US and Canada: sales@matthiasmedia.com
   – in Australia and the rest of the world: sales@matthiasmedia.com.au

Register at our website for our **free** regular email update to receive information about the latest new resources, **exclusive special offers**, and free articles to help you grow in your Christian life and ministry.

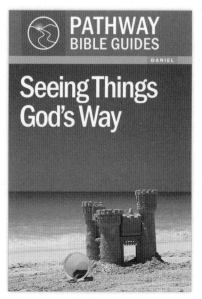

Pathway Bible Guides

athway Bible Guides are simple, straightforward, easy-to-read Bible
udies, ideal for groups who are new to studying the Bible, or groups with
mited time for study. We've designed the studies to be short and easy to
se, with an uncomplicated vocabulary. At the same time, we've tried to
o justice to the passages being studied, and to model good Bible-reading
rinciples. Pathway Bible Guides are simple without being simplistic;
o-nonsense without being no-content.

s of May 2018, the series contains the following titles:

- Beginning with God (Genesis 1-12)
- Getting to Know God (Exodus 1-20)
- One Life Under God (Deuteronomy)
- The Art of Living (Proverbs)
- Under the Sun (Ecclesiastes)
- Seeing Things God's Way (Daniel)
- Return to the Lord (Hosea)
- Fear and Freedom (Matthew 8-12)
- The Unexpected Kingdom (Matthew 13-17)
- Following Jesus (Luke 9-12)
- Peace with God (Romans)
- Church Matters (1 Corinthians 1-7)
- He is Our Peace (Ephesians)
- Fullness in Christ (Colossians)
- Standing Firm (1 Thessalonians)
- Jesus Through Old Testament Eyes
- For Our Sins (The cross)
- Alive with Christ (The resurrection)

FOR MORE INFORMATION OR TO ORDER CONTACT:

Matthias Media
Email: sales@matthiasmedia.com.au
www.matthiasmedia.com.au

Matthias Media (USA)
Email: sales@matthiasmedia.com
www.matthiasmedia.com

From Sinner to Saint

5 studies on holiness for small groups and individuals

From Sinner to Saint is the second in an exciting series of topical Bible studies. Using a mix of Bible investigation, group discussion and video input, From Sinner to Saint will help your group interact with what God is saying about holiness.

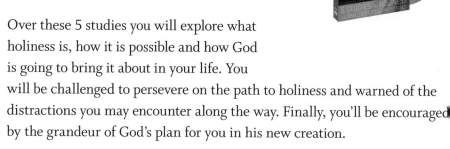

God has a plan. He is transforming every Christian from being a sinner into a saint. That is, God's plan is to make Christians holy, just as he is holy.

Over these 5 studies you will explore what holiness is, how it is possible and how God is going to bring it about in your life. You will be challenged to persevere on the path to holiness and warned of the distractions you may encounter along the way. Finally, you'll be encouraged by the grandeur of God's plan for you in his new creation.

This workbook gives you the road map for each study, with Bible passages to investigate and questions to think through. The accompanying DVD gives you extra input from well-known Bible teacher John Chapman, and will help you tie together the various strands of the Bible's teaching.

FOR MORE INFORMATION OR TO ORDER CONTACT:

Matthias Media
Email: sales@matthiasmedia.com.au
www.matthiasmedia.com.au

Matthias Media (USA)
Email: sales@matthiasmedia.com
www.matthiasmedia.com